Rest for Our Souls

Down-to-Earth
Prayers for Help and Guidance

Nick Fawcett

REST FOR OUR SOULS
Down-to-Earth Prayers for Help and Guidance

Copyright © 2007 Nick Fawcett
Original edition published in English under the title
REST FOR OUR SOULS by Kevin Mayhew Ltd, Buxhall, England.
This edition copyright © Fortress Press 2019

All rights reserved. Except for brief quotations in critical articles or reviews, no part of this book may be reproduced in any manner without prior written permission from the publisher. Email copyright@augsburgfortress.org or write to Permissions, Fortress Press, PO Box 1209, Minneapolis, MN 55440-1209.

The prayers in this book previously appeared in *Touching Down*, *Heaven Touching Earth*, *Touched by His Hand*, and *Touching the Seasons*.

Cover image: Cover art from book interior
Cover design: Tory Herman

Print ISBN: 978-1-5064-5962-2

Contents

- 4 Introduction
- 5 The Sandcastle
- 6 The Long-Distance Truck Driver
- 7 The Tossed Coin
- 8 The Reporter
- 9 The Obstacle Course
- 10 The All-Weather Sports Field
- 11 The Photocopier
- 12 The Solar Eclipse
- 13 The Graffiti
- 14 The Canal Boat
- 15 The Harbor
- 16 The Weather Forecast
- 17 The Fish Tank
- 18 The Swimming Lesson
- 19 The Tree Surgeon
- 20 The Architect's Drawings
- 21 The Bicycle
- 22 The Calculator
- 23 The Motel
- 24 The Relay Race
- 25 The Signpost
- 26 The Tent
- 27 The Carpenter
- 28 The Compass
- 29 The Wet Soap
- 30 The Switch
- 31 The Puzzle Book
- 32 The Maze

Introduction

"Our hearts are restless," observed the medieval theologian St. Augustine, "until they find their rest in God," and his words have struck a chord with generations since. As humans we share a longing for meaning, identity, love, and acceptance—a longing that is as real today as ever. But how should we approach God, and what exactly are we meant to ask for? All too often, when it comes to prayer, words fail us, God seeming remote from daily life.

This book, drawn from four of my recent publications, aims to help answer that conundrum by showing how prayer can spring naturally from everyday experiences—things as ordinary as a signpost, or even a scrawled piece of graffiti. Look at the world more carefully and we will not only hear God speaking but find inspiration for our response. We will begin to recognize that he is all around us—calling, guiding, working, and loving—bringing the fulfilment in life that so many of us seek. I offer this book in the hope that it will not only bring prayer to life but also make life *itself* a prayer.

Nick Fawcett

The Sandcastle

We built it together,
piling up bucket-loads of sand,
building turrets,
constructing walls,
shoring up the defences . . .
but then stood back to watch it fall,
the tide creeping inexorably closer—
nibbling at the edges,
swirling round the base,
and then finally sweeping it away altogether,
as though it had never been.

My life, Lord, is like that,
the happiness I find and goals I strive for
like castles on the beach,
destined to be destroyed;
so much in this world shifting or easily undermined,
here today and gone tomorrow.
Teach me to build wisely,
seeking fulfilment in your love, which, alone,
is able to face the restless tide
and still stand firm
forever.
Amen.

The Long-Distance Truck Driver

He'd driven for miles,
hour upon hour on the highway,
but his journey wasn't over,
not by a long way.
There was still a distance to go,
meaning he'd be traveling again the next day . . .
and the next . . .
the bulk of his life spent on the road.

Remind me, Lord,
that the journey of discipleship isn't over,
however far I may have come;
that each day brings new roads and horizons
to explore,
so much still lying before me.
Save me in this life from ever thinking I've arrived,
but, instead, keep me traveling with you,
until the pilgrimage is over
and I enter your kingdom at last.
Amen.

The Tossed Coin

"Heads," I called,
and heads it was,
the business resolved on the toss of a coin.
Not the best way, perhaps, to settle an issue,
but in this case it did the job—
a simple matter
simply resolved.

I wish all choices were that easy, Lord,
as swift and straightforward to deal with,
but they're not,
most being far more complex—
what seems right to some seeming wrong to others.
Give me wisdom, then, in all my decisions,
and, above all, the courage I need
both to make them
and to amend them when I get them wrong.
Amen.

The Reporter

She was there on the scene,
swift to report the facts—
to pass on, as best she could,
everything she'd seen and heard—
her story not simply gleaned from others
and cobbled together
but written on the spot:
an eyewitness account as events unfolded.

Teach me, Lord, to witness authentically to you,
speaking from personal experience
of what I've found to be true.
Help me to bring to life the reality of your love,
telling of the blessings you've given,
guidance offered,
mercy shown,
and peace imparted.
You have given me good news,
glad tidings for all.
Help me to share it.
Amen.

The Obstacle Course

It was a challenge, no doubt about that—
walls to scale,
water to cross,
ropes to climb,
tunnels to negotiate—
but, grueling though it was
and exhausted though they often felt,
they stuck at it,
tenaciously surmounting every obstacle
in their resolve to complete the course.

Teach me, Lord, to persevere,
not discouraged by the obstacles I meet along the way
but recognizing them as integral to the course,
each a new challenge, to be faced with you.
However stiff the test or depleted my reserves,
help me to battle on
and run my race to the very end.
Amen.

The All-Weather Sports Field

The wind blew and heavens opened,
but though all around rain stopped play,
they carried on with their game,
for the field was built to withstand the elements,
summer or winter,
day or night—
ready, in all conditions,
like the players themselves,
for play to continue.

Forgive me, Lord,
for though I speak of commitment,
mine's a fair-weather discipleship,
strong enough when the sun shines,
but swift to founder should the wind blow cold.
Give me a faith for all seasons,
as true to you in calm or storm
as you are true to me.
Amen.

The Photocopier

It ran off the copies in no time,
each of them perfect,
an exact replica of the one before—
so simple yet so effective—
achieving in minutes
what it would have taken me hours to do by hand.

Lord, you do not expect me to be just like you,
and you do not want all your people to be clones,
each thinking and acting the same,
but you *do* want something of Christ to show
in the lives of those who follow you.
Work within me,
so that, despite all that mars the picture,
at least a little of his love, joy, and goodness
may shine through.
Amen.

The Solar Eclipse

It was a strange moment,
a once-in-a-lifetime experience—
fascinating yet strangely eerie,
the world for a moment going dark,
shadow replacing sunshine,
night usurping day.
But then it was over,
the light returning once more,
seemingly brighter than ever.

Remind me, Lord, when shadows darken my life
and light seems suddenly extinguished,
that you entered the darkness of death
and rose victorious;
that you experienced the full force of hatred
and conquered it with love;
that you took on the powers of evil
and worked through them for good.
Remind me, then, that your light will always shine,
nothing in heaven or earth finally able to overcome it.
Amen.

The Graffiti

The wall was covered,
obliterated by a hodgepodge of words and pictures,
some smutty,
others obscene,
a few touched by humor,
most driven by hate,
yet all springing from a common desire
to leave some mark;
to shout defiantly to the world:
"I was here!"

What mark will I leave, Lord, when my course is run?
What imprint will I have made,
not on bricks and mortar
but on human hearts?
Help me to live in such a way
that my words and deeds speak of you,
testament not to my brief span but to your eternal love,
and may that be legacy enough.
Amen.

The Canal Boat

I'd have been faster walking,
our progress leisurely to say the least,
but in that lay its charm,
for this was a trip to be savored,
celebrated,
taking in the sights and sounds along the way—
the journey as much a pleasure as the destination.

Teach me, Lord,
though my destination lies beyond this world,
to celebrate the journey of life,
recognizing the innumerable ways
it can fill me with joy,
touch me with wonder,
and move me to gratitude.
Save me from being so full of heaven
that I lose sight of earth,
from dwelling so much on joys to come
that I close my eyes to blessings now.
You offer life in all its fullness.
Teach me to live it now.
Amen.

The Harbor

It offered welcome respite from the worst of the storm,
boats hurrying for shelter
from the howling gale and surging waves,
but when conditions improved
they were soon on their way,
out again into open water
and about their business once more.

Lord, though you promise shelter when the wind blows,
a haven in times of turmoil,
save me from divorcing faith from life,
as though commitment involves running away
from the world
and the challenges it brings.
May moments of retreat and quiet devotion
inspire me rather to fresh service
and new ventures in faith.
Amen.

The Weather Forecast

"Showers dying out from the west,
followed by sunny intervals with a gentle breeze"—
isn't that what he said?
It's not what we got, though—
nothing like it.
It's poured since this morning
and is still blowing a gale now,
the most we've had just a brief burst of sunshine,
a tantalizing glimpse of what might have been.

Lord, we can try to plan ahead,
predict the future,
and yes, at times, make a decent attempt at it,
but in things that really matter,
life-shaping events and issues,
we can rarely be confident,
still less sure.
Teach us that, though we may map our intended path,
it is you who directs our steps,
and you alone who holds the future in your hands.
Amen.

The Fish Tank

They darted this way and that,
probing, foraging, and exploring,
secure in their own little world.
Were they aware of me looking in,
conscious of another plane,
an altogether different dimension,
beyond the boundaries that confined them?

There's so much, Lord, that I don't see,
the world of my senses not the whole story
but just a glimpse of reality,
one aspect of a greater whole.
Save me from being bound by my limited horizons,
closing my life to wonders beyond
and riches yet to be revealed.
Open my heart to your infinite love,
greater than eye has seen or mind conceived.
Amen.

The Swimming Lesson

I was scared, Lord,
scared of lifting my feet off the bottom
and trusting myself to the water.
I knew what I had to do,
and could see others around me doing it—
the thought of going under
never even entering their heads.
But theory was one thing,
practice another.
It needed a leap of faith,
and I was afraid to make it.

Lord, I don't find faith in *you* any easier.
Though I talk blithely enough about it,
when it comes to the moment of truth,
to letting go and trusting you,
I'm as nervous as a kitten,
testing the water but no more,
and thus failing either to sink or swim.
Give me the courage I need to take the plunge
and place my all in your hands.
Amen.

The Tree Surgeon

It seemed drastic surgery,
almost brutal,
virtually every branch lopped off,
leaving a denuded trunk;
it was hard to believe such a sorry sight
could shoot again—
that fresh growth,
new life,
could burst out of the old.
Yet, just a few months later, there it was—
the tree back in leaf,
fully restored to its former glory.

Prune the deadwood from my life, Lord,
and all redundant growth.
Though the process may be painful
and the measures severe,
trim back whatever undermines true health
and wholeness,
so that I may reach greater maturity in faith
and become more fully the person you want me to be.
Amen.

The Architect's Drawings

They gave a picture of what might be,
a sense of how something old and dilapidated
could be transformed,
new life breathed into it,
potential hidden for so long at last unlocked.
It would take time, of course,
effort too,
but if the will was there,
then the goal could be reached,
the dream realized.

You offer in Christ, Lord, a picture of what *life* can be,
what *I* can be—
everything made new—
yet I struggle to believe it possible,
for I fall so far short
and find it hard to change even a little.
Teach me that,
provided I'm serious about commitment
and prepared to play my part,
you can do what *I* can't—
to fashion a new creation
from the unpromising material of my life.
Amen.

The Bicycle

"Have faith," they said.
"Look up,
keep pedaling,
you'll be fine."
But I didn't believe them,
for it didn't make sense,
the bike falling even as they spoke.
I wobbled . . .
toppled . . .
and fell.

"Try again," they said.
"You'll crack it eventually,
you'll see."
So I got back on,
that time . . .
and the next . . .
and the next . . .
until eventually I not only stayed on,
but did so without thinking,
cycling suddenly seeming as natural as breathing.

Lord, even when it's hard,
everything seeming to count against it,
teach me to keep faith,
knowing that, however much I falter,
and however hard I fall,
you will lift me up and set me back on my way.
Amen.

The Calculator

He tapped in the numbers, one after the other,
and came up with the right result,
down to the tenth decimal point,
but he'd little idea how he'd got there,
his grasp of mathematics minimal.
Having never grasped the essentials for himself,
stripped of the calculator he'd be lost.

Lord, in terms of Christian belief
I can come up with the right answers,
but unless I've experienced the truth for myself
that ability counts for little.
Teach me to know you personally
instead of relying on the perception of others;
to work *out* my faith
and *at* my discipleship,
so that it all makes sense for *me*.
Amen.

The Motel

It wasn't the place for a holiday,
still less where I'd choose to live,
but it was clean, comfortable, and convenient,
ideal for those looking to break their journey.

Remind me, Lord,
that in this world I'm merely passing through;
that, for all its beauty and wonder—
the countless joys it has to offer—
it's not my final destination
but a staging post along the way.
Teach me, then, to celebrate everything it has to offer,
yet not to be bound by it,
to savor its many riches,
but never to confuse them with blessings still to come.
Amen.

The Relay Race

They were running superbly,
a gold medal in sight;
just one more changeover to make
and victory was theirs,
triumph assured.
But then, disaster . . .
the baton fumbled . . .
dropped . . .
and the race was lost.

You call me in turn, Lord,
to pass the baton on to others,
handing on to them the message I've received,
but too often I betray that trust,
keeping to myself what I should have shared,
going it alone and forgetting the bigger picture.
Forgive me
and help me to play my part in your purpose,
running my leg of the race faithfully,
so that others may run theirs in turn.
Amen.

The Signpost

It was such a relief to see it:
to know, after hours of wandering
and repeated detours,
that we were back on track—
with miles to go still, admittedly,
but at least headed in the right direction,
on course to reach our goal.

Show me the way *I* should go, Lord,
for so often I lose my bearings,
willfully taking the wrong road
or wandering aimlessly through life.
When I mistake the path or stray from it,
remind me that you are the way that leads to life,
and may that knowledge guide my footsteps.
Amen.

The Tent

It wasn't a palace,
far from it,
but it was a place to bed down for the night.
And when we were ready to move on,
it could be rolled up,
packed away,
and carried with us;
not an encumbrance
but an aid to our journey,
integral to our travels.

Remind me, Lord, that discipleship is a journey—
not a destination—
about moving forward:
exploring fresh horizons,
discovering new possibilities,
and experiencing yet more of your love.
Save me from getting stuck in a spiritual rut,
settling for what is comfortable and familiar.
Teach me instead to let go of whatever holds me back
and to venture out in faith,
open to whatever you hold in store.
Amen.

The Carpenter

I watched spellbound as he worked:
taking the rough-hewn block of wood
and turning it on the lathe,
sculpting and shaping it with gouge and chisel,
painstakingly transforming the ordinary
into a work of art.

And I thought, Lord, of the carpenter's son,
learning his trade in Nazareth;
of *your* Son,
nailed to a rough-hewn cross;
of the young man leaving his father's workshop
to build instead his Father's kingdom,
fashioning not just timber but human lives.

Fashion me now, Lord, by the touch of your hand,
and finish your new creation.
Take who I am,
and from the deadwood of my life
craft something beautiful for you.
Amen.

The Compass

It didn't tell me exactly where I was,
or spell out the path to follow,
but it helped me get my bearings—
enough to work out the next step,
the direction I should take.
And though the way wasn't always easy
or the path always clear,
it was sufficient for my needs,
leading me safely to my final destination.

Thank you, Lord, for the guidance you offer each day,
not setting out detailed instructions
for every aspect of life,
still less dictating the course I should take,
but prompting through your word
and pointing the way forward.
Teach me to travel in faith until the journey is done,
your love a light to my path,
a compass through the changing scenes of life.
Amen.

The Wet Soap

I grabbed it
and grabbed it again,
like a novice juggler learning his trade,
but the soap was wet
and it fell from my grasp,
too slippery to hold.

So much in life is the same, Lord:
impossible to hold on to.
I think it's mine,
safely secured,
only for it to slip away—
here one minute and gone the next.
Teach me to celebrate the joys of this world
but to root my happiness in what lies beyond it—
in your love that never ends
and that nothing can take away.
Amen.

The Switch

I left it switched on,
even though I was going away,
and when I returned a few days later
the batteries were dead,
drained of all power,
no good for anything
until they had been fully recharged.

I forget, Lord, that I too need to switch off sometimes
if I'm not to end up exhausted.
Teach me to appreciate the importance of being still,
of taking a breather from the demands of life,
however pressing they may be.
Show me the difference between doing enough
and doing too much,
and help me to get the balance right.
Amen.

The Puzzle Book

I could work some out easily enough,
but not others.
They left me scratching my head,
sitting with furrowed brow,
bemused and frustrated.
There was an answer somewhere, of course,
a solution to them all,
but what it was
and how to get there
eluded me completely.

So much in life, Lord, leaves me equally baffled,
hard to square with faith or reconcile with your love.
Tragedy, pain, injustice, and evil cause me to flounder,
searching in vain for a credible explanation.
Are there answers, Lord?
I believe so,
and I'll keep on seeking understanding,
but help me in the meantime to live with questions,
and to keep faith despite them all.
Amen.

The Maze

I knew where I was going . . .
or so I thought . . .
mastering the twists and turns a piece of cake,
barely a challenge at all.
But suddenly there was no way through,
and I found myself retracing my steps,
coming up against one blind alley after another,
until, hard though I kept on trying,
there was no avoiding the truth:
I was lost.

When it comes to life, Lord,
despite the maze of options that daily confronts me,
I feel confident of taking the right path
and negotiating my way safely through the labyrinth.
Yet plans have a habit of going astray,
few things working out as I would like;
so, time and again, I end up lost and confused,
uncertain where to turn next.
In all the complexities each day brings,
the moral and ethical dilemmas,
the confusing choices and life-shaping decisions,
grant me your guidance and see me safely through.
Amen.

www.ingramcontent.com/pod-product-compliance
Lightning Source LLC
Chambersburg PA
CBHW052038070526
44584CB00020B/3156